HTML & CSS:
A Beginner's Guide

MITESH DABHI

Copyright © 2013 Mitesh Dabhi

ISBN-10: 1500501840
ISBN-13: 978-1500501846

TO BINAL

CONTENTS

Preface

Welcome to the first edition of *HTML & CSS: A Beginner's Guide*. When I first started writing this guide, I thought to myself, *Yet another HTML book – do I really need to do this?* I learnt HTML and CSS by practice from books on loan from my local library 10 years ago. Back then the Web was in its infancy and 56K dial-up modems were the norm. Since then, I hadn't even looked at other HTML books. But after doing some research recently, I read through several HTML books in the marketplace that were too complicated for the average reader. I felt compelled to write a book that gives readers an easy-to-use way to learn the basics of HTML (short for "Hypertext Markup Language") and CSS (or "Cascading Style Sheets").

HTML & CSS: A Beginner's Guide is a book I wish I'd had when I learnt HTML. It offers practical guidance, examples and know-how without the long boring technical fluff. It will teach you what you need to know and how to apply it to related Web development issues.

HTML is a "markup language" (a term used in Web-page design) that lets you create Web pages by combining text and graphics using special instructions. CSS is used with HTML to control the style and the appearance of a Web page such as fonts, colors and layout. (We will go into more detail on how to use CSS in the second part of this guide.)

Quite simply, HTML tells a browser how to display and format text on a Web page. And to create that Web page all you really need is a simple text editor such as Windows Notepad (which you can find in your Windows Start menu) and the basic tools presented in this guide.

Hypertext Markup Language – HTML – is the underlying structure of the World Wide Web. It's the common single thread that connects each and every Web site on the Internet – from a large corporate Web site to a single classroom project at your local grade school.

Don't let the thought of learning HTML intimidate you. It's not rocket science, but like learning anything new, it does take a bit of practice to gain an understanding of it.

You also don't need any prior computer programming or Web development experience to learn HTML. It's very easy to get started – in fact, in a matter of minutes you can create a Web page and view it in on the Web.

Before we dive into the actual creation of Web pages, you'll need to understand a few things about the World Wide Web.

Chapter 1

Understanding the World Wide Web

The World Wide Web is the name that is given to a specific part of the Internet that you can access from the comfort of your home or office using Web browser software. (Currently, Google Chrome, Internet Explorer and Mozilla Firefox are the three most dominant Web browsers online.) Normally the words *Internet* and *World Wide Web* are used interchangeably to describe the Web. But to be more accurate, the Internet and the Web are two separate but related things. By the end of this chapter you'll know the difference between these two.

What is an ISP?

An **Internet service provider** (**ISP**, also called **Internet access provider**) is a business that offers user's access to the Internet and related services for a fee. Many ISPs are telephone companies or other telecommunication companies, such as AOL, BT, TalkTalk, and Virgin Media. A "browser" is a software program that runs on your personal computer and allows you to navigate and view Web pages. The most popular browsers are Mozilla Firefox, Google Chrome and Internet Explorer. A "server" is a computer, running special software, which is always connected to the Internet.

What Is the Internet?

The Internet is a global network of computers connected together by telephone lines, cables and satellites. When you connect *your* computer to the Internet through your Internet Service Provider (ISP), you are part of the ISP's network, which is connected to the Internet. Similar to the postal system enabling people to send mail, the Internet allows computers to talk to one another.

On the Internet, computers send tiny packets of data to one another using a common language called Transmission Control/Internet Protocol or TCP/IP. It's essentially a unique identity for the computer, like your home address. Every computer connected to the Internet is given an IP address.

An Internet Protocol – or IP – is simply a set of rules that allows computers to talk to one another by exchanging data. If you're an experienced old-timer, you may have come across these IPs on your adventures around the Web:

HTTP (Hypertext Transfer Protocol). Transmits hypertext over computer networks. This is the standard protocol of the World Wide Web.

SMTP (Simple Mail Transfer Protocol) for email. Transfers email messages and attachments to electronic mailboxes.

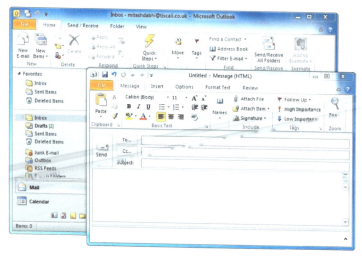

VoIP (Voice Over Internet Protocol). Allows for delivery of voice communications over the Web – for example, Skype phone calls.

How Does the Internet Work?

When you send a package or letter by post, you don't need to know the details about how it's getting to its destination or how many post offices it may pass through on the way. Similarly, when you send an email or other electronic file on your computer, you don't need to know how many packets of data are being sent through telephone lines, cables, routers, satellites and servers (host computers) on your email's way to its final destination.

Those packages and letters you send by post may also contain different types of information: a letter, an invoice for a recent transaction on eBay, a photograph or a job application. In the same way, the Internet's data packets can also carry different types of data: Web pages, email messages, music files, digital videos and even computer programs.

Today's Web offers a friendly, convenient and easy-to-use interface for browsing and accessing information online. But before the invention of Web browsing software, it was necessary to know how to use text commands in a command-line interface (or operating system) like MS-DOS to make things happen.

```
C:\>Dir
```

Fig 1-1: MS-DOS command prompt

Figure 1-1 shows a MS-DOS command prompt. The Dir command stands for directory and will display a list.

What Is the Web?

The World Wide Web – commonly known as the Web or WWW for short – is a part of the Internet that consists of millions of Web sites (like Amazon.com, Ebay.com, Yahoo.com and Facebook.com) and billions of Web pages. In fact, a Web site is simply a collection of Web *pages* that are linked together using hyperlinks.

A hyperlink is an electronic text link within a Web page that is distinctly set off from the other text around it. Hyperlinks are usually underlined and highlighted in a blue color. Graphics and images can also be used as hyperlinks. When you hover over hyperlink text or graphics with your mouse, the pointer changes to a hand to indicate the text or graphic is a hyperlink and clicking on a hyperlink will take you to a new Web page or Web site. Hyperlinks are essentially used to navigate to other pages of a Web site or to the Web in general. Think of hyperlink navigation like this: When you open a book, you just don't jump to any random page and start reading; first you look at the table of contents, and then you find the chapter you want. A hyperlink works in exactly the same way.

A Web page is similar to a word processing document

because it too can contain text, images, sounds, animations and video. If you know how to create a word processing document using a program like Word, then you can create a simple Web page.

Anatomy of a Web Page: What's a URL?

A URL (pronounced U-R-L) is a fancy way of saying Web page address. The letters URL stand for Uniform Resource Locator. You can navigate to a Web page by typing its URL into the address bar of your Web browser. The following illustration shows an example of a URL in Mozilla Firefox.

You've probably never heard of a Web address being referred to as a URL, but you have seen URL addresses. They start with **http://**, and end with **.com**, **.org**, **.edu** or **.net**.

Every Web page on the Internet has a Web site address or URL. For example, http://www.google.com is the Web site address for Google's home page. Let's use that address to explain the parts of a URL.

The Parts of a URL

A URL is composed of many parts that each make up a Web site address like this one:

http://www.google.com

The first part of the URL in our example – *http://* – is a protocol (a rule working behind the scenes for transmitting data) used in the communication between your Web browser and the server (host computer) on the Internet. The letters stand for Hypertext Transfer Protocol. When you enter 'http' into your Web browser, it lets the server know that you want to access Web mode using this protocol. There are also other protocols for transferring files (FTP or File Transfer Protocol) or transferring email message (SMTP or Simple Mail Transfer Protocol) amongst many others.

The second part of the URL – *www.google.com* – identifies the host name of the server you are connecting to on the Web. In this URL, you are asking to see a file located on the Google server. As mentioned earlier, WWW is an acronym for World Wide Web, but it's not necessary to type it in an address any longer as most Web servers don't need it to navigate to the site you want.

So, to sum it all up, the URL in the example says it would like to use the HTTP protocol to connect to a server on the Internet called **www.google.com.** In Chapter 2, "Create Your First Web Page" you'll learn about the elements that make up a Web Page.

Chapter 2

Creating Your First Web Page

What Is HTML?

HTML, short for Hypertext Markup Language, is a language for creating and describing Web pages on the World Wide Web. It's the standard language of the Web. But unlike other computer programming languages, it's free and you don't have to pay for a software license to use it.

An HTML page is made up of groups of tags enclosed in angled brackets (< >).. If you crack open an HTML file, you will see a mixture of HTML tags and plain text characters (like letters, numbers, special characters, and punctuation marks).

HTML is basically a set of instructions (tags and text) telling the browser how text, images and graphics are displayed on the page. The browser doesn't display these tags, but simply interprets them to display the contents of the Web page. Put another way, HTML is actually a set of commands that tell the browser what to do. For example, a Web page may include a command instructing a browser to display text as the main heading within a document. That command would look like this:

<h1>Welcome to my home page</h1>

Here the <h1> Welcome to my home page </h1> tag is essentially telling the Web browser that the text is a main heading in a HTML document and should be set on its own line; </h1> indicates the end of the tag.

A Brief History of HTML

As we said earlier, HTML is the foundation of every Web site on the World Wide Web. It was invented by the British scientist Tim Berners-Lee in 1989. At the time he was working as a contractor at CERN – short for *Conseil Européen pour la Recherche* Nucléaire or the European Organisation for Nuclear Research – in Switzerland.

As part of his job, Berners-Lee needed to share information with other physicists. To his surprise he discovered that there was no simple, quick and easy way to do that. Not only did you have to log into many different computers to get bits and pieces of information, but you had to learn how to use a complicated operating system for *each* of those computers: the scientists at CERN came from universities around the world, and they brought with them all types of computers. Not only were there UNIX, Mac and PC operating systems to deal with, but also mainframe and medium-sized computers running all sorts of software.

To solve the problem of communicating between computers with different operating systems and software, Berners-Lee wrote a program to help him keep track of important documents and files by using a series of links (hypertext). Using his hypertext program, he connected these documents and files together like an index in a book. He originally named the program "Enquire," after a book he loved to read in his childhood. Back then, his program was capable of storing information and connecting documents electronically, but you could only access this information from one computer at a time.

In 1989 Berners-Lee took a giant leap towards his vision of a global system where documents could be linked via hypertext to the Internet, allowing people from around the globe to share and link information with each other regardless of the computer or software they used. He named his project the "World Wide Web."

At the time, many people thought that the idea of connecting documents stored on computers around the world was too ambitious and impossible. In the beginning, in fact, no one was interested in Berners-Lee's idea except for a few colleagues who supported and nurtured his vision. So under their guidance he went on to develop the four critical foundations of the Web: the language of the World Wide Web (HTML); the hypertext system for linking documents together (HTTP); the system for locating documents on the web (the URL); and the first graphic user interface (Web browser). In 1991, the Web as we now know it was launched and immediately took off.

Getting Started: Using the View Source Command of Your Browser

A fantastic way to learn HTML is to surf the Web and look under the hood of the Web sites that you like (and the ones that you don't like as well). Remember, that by doing this you will become familiar with what source code looks like.

Most Web browsers will let you view the HTML source code of a Web site. Open up your Internet browser and then surf to a Web page whose source code you'd like to view. In Google Chrome, for example, surf to the Web page you want and choose **Tools | View Source** from the main menu. In Microsoft Internet Explorer, go to your Web page and choose **View | Source** (see below).

File	Edit	View	Favorites	Tools	Help

Toolbars	▶
Quick tabs	Ctrl+Q
Explorer bars	▶
Go to	▶
Stop	Esc
Refresh	F5
Zoom (100%)	▶
Text size	▶
Encoding	▶
Style	▶
Caret browsing	F7
Source	Ctrl+U
Security report	
International website address	
Webpage privacy policy...	
Full screen	F11

When viewing Web page source code, you will see many HTML tags with plain text characters, letters, numbers, special characters and punctuation marks enclosed in angled brackets (< >). The most common tags you will come across are (<h1>) headings, (<b>) boldface, and (<p>) paragraphs. Later on in the next chapter, you will be using these as you create your own web page.

As you study the HTML source code, you'll notice other types of code in the document. For instance, apart from the standard HTML code, you might also find references to other files, documents or servers.

Creating an HTML File

An HTML file is made up of groups of tags. A tag is a set of instructions telling the Web browser how to display content on a page. An HTML tag is usually enclosed in an angled bracket like this: < >. The HTML code sits between these brackets. For example, a simple tag is the <b> tag, which stands for "bold." This command basically tells the browser to apply bold formatting to text. Here is an example of text with and without tags:

This text is not bold. **<b>This text is bold.</b>**

So, instead of clicking a button to make text bold, italic or underline – as you would with a word processing program like Word – you have to type out a tag to apply formatting to text in HTML.

Note in the example above that HTML tags come in pairs, and most tags have a starting tag and an ending tag. For example, the starting tag **(<b>)** switches on an effect (bold lettering), and the ending tag **(</b>) switches off the effect. Also note that the ending tag is set off by a forward slash (/) that "closes" the tag.** You *always* have to close your tags, or the Web browser will not format the page.

Using Windows Notepad to Create an HTML File

To create a basic HTML file, you don't need any special software or expensive training. We'll be using Windows Notepad. It's free, it comes with every copy of Windows 7, and it's really very easy to use as you'll soon see.

1. Click on the Start menu and then browse to Windows Notepad. The quickest way to get there is to click on the Start menu, then All Programs, then Accessories. You'll find the Windows Notepad application listed in here.

2. Click on the Notepad application to launch it. You'll now see a blank window ready for you to start typing in.

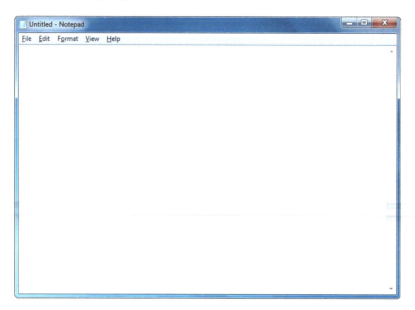

3. (*Optional Step*): Normally, Windows will hide the file extensions of well-known file types. For example, a file named "home.html" will be shown as "home" without its file extension. It can be quite confusing, so let's go ahead and change these options

To do this, you will need to open the Folder Options menu. Begin by clicking on the Start button, then Control Panel, then Appearance and Personalization; then click on Folder Options.

Go to the View tab and scroll down until you see an option for "Hide extensions for known file types" and **uncheck** this option (see the screenshot below). Click "OK" to save your preferences and you'll now see all the file extensions in Windows.

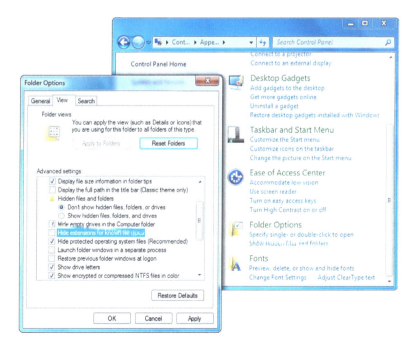

Before you start creating your first HTML Web page, create a new empty folder on your desktop and call it "HTML." This folder is where you will be saving your HTML files.

4. Now return to your blank Notepad window (see Step 2 above). Start by typing this basic text into the Notepad window: "This is my first web page."

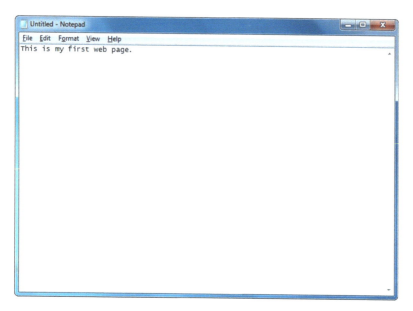

5. Once you've done this, save your file. To do this, choose File and then click Save As. You'll see a Save As dialogue box pop up. Save your file with the name "Index.html" to the HTML folder that you just created in Step 2. Remember to type in the file extension **.html so that** your file will be saved as a Web page. If you forget to add the file extension, Notepad will just save your file as a plain text character file.

File Names and File Extensions

An HTML file is simply an ordinary text file, which you create and name, that ends with an **.html** or **.htm** file extension. **(The .htm extension is equivalent to the .html one, but .html is used more frequently.)** A file extension is a three- or four-letter suffix, preceded by a period (.), which follows your file's name. So, if you create an HTML file that you name **Index**, the full file name would look like this: Index.html. File extensions generally indicate what type of file a document or item is and the software application needed to open it. Other file extensions you are probably familiar with include **.doc** or **.docx** for Microsoft Word documents and **.jpg** for an image or a photograph file.

Preview Your File in a Web Browser

Once you've saved your HTML file you can preview it in your Web browser on your computer. For this you don't have to be connected to the Internet to view your files.

When you want to preview your file, go to the folder where you saved your work. Open your Web browser, choose File | Open and navigate to your folder where you saved your HTML file.

As you begin to develop more confidence, you will want to make changes to your HTML file. Simply browse to the location where your file has been saved on your computer. Select the file and then right click Edit with Notepad.

To view the changes you've made in your Web browser, you'll have to click the Refresh or Reload button in your browser. It's also a good idea to keep both programs (Notepad and your Web browser) open at the same time as you go along as you can easily make changes and preview them.

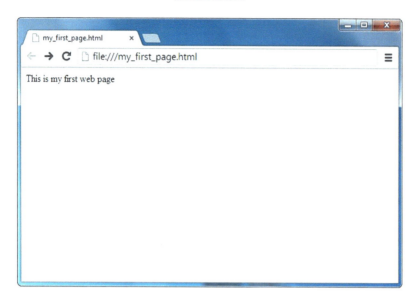

Chapter 3

Formatting Your Web Page

By now you're more familiar with HTML (Hypertext Markup Language). As we said earlier, HTML is the underlying structure of the World Wide Web, and a Web page is made up of sets of HTML markup tags that tell a browser how to display Web page text. In this chapter, you'll learn how to structure a plain HTML document with markup tags.

Your First "Proper" Web Page

All HTML pages will contain an <html>, <head>, <title>, and <body> tag – with a **<!DOCTYPE>** declaration specified at the very beginning of the document. (The doctype declaration tells your browser what kind of markup language you are using in the document. In our examples, the language is HTML.)

When learning a new programming language, it's always been customary to display the words "Hello World" on the computer screen. It's a programming-learning tradition to use the simple computer program "Hello World" to demonstrate to beginners the basic syntax of a programming language.

To begin, we are going to display the words "Hello World" on an HTML page within an Internet browser. You don't need any special software to do this; a simple text editor will do. Here we are using Windows Notepad, but if you're using a Mac, TextEdit is just as good.

Create a new document in your text editor of choice. Just type it in exactly as you see here:

```
<!doctype html>
<html>
<head>
<title>My First Web Page</title>
</head>
<body>
Hello World...
</body>
```

Once you've done this save your file with the name **myfirstpage.html** in your HTML folder.

A **doctype identifier** always begins with an exclamation mark and is always placed at the start of a document, before the <html> tag. The doctype identifier essentially tells the Web browser which standard (special instruction) your page is following. The doctype identifier we have used in the example above is the new HTML5 doctype. It tells the Web browser that the language used is HTML. (Earlier versions of HTML used longer, more complex doctype declarations – for example: <!DOCTYPE HTML PUBLIC "-//W3C//DTD HTML 4.01//EN" "HTTP://w3.org/TR/HTML4/STRICT.DTD">.)

The **<html>** tag tells a Web browser that it is looking at an HTML document. It's a basic container that wraps the other elements in your Web page. A container is an area enclosed with the beginning and closing tags. Text contained between **<html>** and **</html>** normally enclose the whole document

The **<head>** tag is a container for the header section of your HTML document. Here it includes the title of our web page Text contained between **<head>** and **</head>** simply

18

tells the Web browser general information about the document.

The **<title>** tag is needed in all of our HTML documents. It's the name or title of our Web page, which a browser displays on its title bar. A title is also displayed when you bookmark a Web page to your "favorites" toolbar and when you surf the Web looking for a specific page in Google.

The **<body>** tag is a container for the actual contents of your Web page. This can include headings, text, hyperlinks, images, tables and lists. To display actual content on your Web page you must always place it inside the **<body>** tag of your page.

Congratulations, you've just created your first Web page. If you preview your document in a Web browser you'll find the page displaying the words "Hello World" on screen (as shown in Figure 3-1).

Fig 3-1: Hello World displayed in your Web browser

Adding Basic Content

Every Web page needs a container for the text to be displayed within the **<body>** section of our page. This text container is the paragraph **<p>** tag.

Here is the **<p>** tag added to our Web page:

```
<!doctype html>
<html>
<head>
<title>My First Web Page</title>
</head>
<body>
<p>Hello World...</p>
</body>
</html>
```

The **<p>** tag tells the browser to add a paragraph. Web browsers usually don't indent paragraphs but add a little space between each paragraph before and after each paragraph tag.

Before going any further, open up the Web page we created earlier in Windows Notepad (myfirstpage.html) and add the **<p>** tag to it. Remember to close the tag with **</p>**.

Every Web page uses this bare-bones skeleton, and you can now use this as a template whenever you create a new HTML document.

WYSIWYG Editors

At some point you'll begin to wonder: Why should I go through the trouble of learning HTML when a What You See Is What You Get (WYSIWG) editor can do it for me? It's a great question, and is often the case; it is much easier to create a Web site using WYSIWYG editor as you don't need to have an understanding of HTML.

WYSIWYG editors don't require you to know any HTML. Instead of looking at HTML code, you can basically drag and drop pieces of your Web page as you see fit. You also have the ability to preview how your Web page will look like in a Web browser.

It's very easy creating a Web page using a WYSIWYG editor. But if you don't have an understanding of HTML and things go wrong, you'll struggle trying to fix your Web pages. That's why it's essential to learn HTML. Once you've grasped the basics of HTML, you can experiment with WYSIWYG editors. The most popular WYSIWYG editors are

- **Adobe Dreamweaver** is available on both the Macintosh and the PC. This program is the industry standard known for its advanced features and extensive coding capabilities.

- **Microsoft Expression Web** is only available on the PC. However Microsoft Expression boasts compliant standards code and CSS (Cascading Style Sheets) based layouts.

HTML editors

HTML editors basically speed up the process of writing HTML code by hand. You can't edit Web pages visually like WYSIWYG editors, however many Web Designers prefer to write HTML documents by hand. The most popular HTML editors are

- **Sublime Text 2** this advanced text editor is available on both the PC and Macintosh. A beautiful clean text editor has a $70 license fee but you can use it as it boasts an unlimited trial offer.

- **Notepad (Windows)** Notepad is a simple plain text code editor for Windows.

Get Your Tools

Now fire up your web browser, roll up your sleeves and then

go to the following Web page to download and install **Sublime Text 2**.

```
http://www.sublimetext.com
```

After you've downloaded the file, simply launch it on your PC (This program will self-install automatically on your operating system.) You can still continue to use Windows Notepad to write HTML code however Sublime Text 2 is a proper text/code editor which has been specifically designed for this very purpose.

I personally prefer using Sublime Text 2 as it color codes my HTML code and it's really easy to distinguish tags within the document (as shown in Fig 3-2).

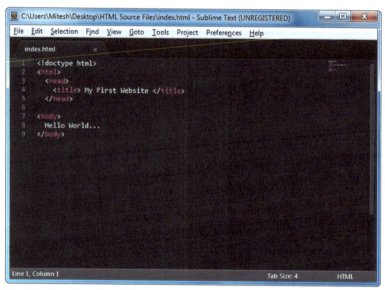

Fig 3-2: Sublime Text 2

Chapter 4

Text Elements

Now that you've learnt how to create a very basic and simple Web page in HTML, it's time to start learning how to add content to your page. In a traditional word processing program such as Word, it's very easy to change the size of a font, text color or typeface, and make paragraph and spacing changes. You simply click on the Word menu's formatting options. But with HTML it's more complicated to make such changes. Instead, you have to tell a Web browser *how* to format your document. Let's start with paragraphs.

Paragraphs

In most word processing programs you can simply hit the return or Enter key on your keyboard to create a new paragraph in your document. But that won't work for HTML: Web browsers are designed to ignore the line breaks you create when you hit the enter key.

To create a paragraph, you have to use the paragraph **<p>** tag. Every time you begin a new line of text in your HTML document, always add the **<p>** | **</p>** tag to act as a container for your content (A container is an area surrounded with the start and closing tags). See the example below:

<p> here is my text for a paragraph. </p>
<p> here is my next paragraph. </p>

The **<p>** tag tells a Web browser that a paragraph has been defined in the body section of the document. Whenever you begin a new paragraph in your document you must always use the **<p>** tag.

Line Breaks

Sometimes you want to add a new line of text to your HTML document by hitting the return or Enter key on your keyboard – but you *don't* want to create a new paragraph, because your Web browser will add extra spaces between your paragraphs. Let's say, for example, you're writing a poem and you want to tightly control where each line ends. To do that, you need to use the HTML line break tag **
** like this:

> **<p>**Do you remember still the falling stars**
**
> that like swift horses through the**
**
> heavens raced and suddenly leaped**
**
> across the hurdles of our wishes – do**
**
> you recall? And we did make so many**
**
> **</p>**

Line breaks (the **br** stands for **break**) will tell a Web browser to force a single line return in your HTML document. The **
** is what programmers call an "empty tag," which means you don't have to close it using the forward slash (for example, </br>), as you do with most tags. Other examples of common "empty tags" include: <meta>, <img> and <hr>.

Headings

Headings are titles of sections just above paragraphs like the one above ("Headings"). A heading in a printed document tells you what the page is all about. Headings in your HTML documents are similar to what you might use in a word processing document such as Word. Web browsers also display headings in bold, and at various sizes, depending on the HTML heading level specified. HTML defines six levels of headings, beginning with **<h1>** (the biggest) and ending with **<h6>** (the smallest). Let's create a new HTML document that displays HTML's different settings.

24

Create a new document in Sublime Text 2 by selecting File | New. Now type the code exactly as you see here:

```
<!doctype html>
<html>
  <head>
  <title> Headings </title>
  <meta charset="UTF-8" />
  </head>
<body>
  <h1> Heading 1 </h1>
  <h2> Heading 2 </h2>
  <h3> Heading 3 </h3>
  <h4> Heading 4 </h4>
  <h5> Heading 5 </h5>
  <h6> Heading 6 </h6>
</body>
</html>
```

Once you've done this save your file with the name "Headings.html" in your HTML folder on your desktop. Then preview your page in your Web browser to check your work.

The **<meta charset="utf-8">** tag tells the browser what character encoding to use in our Web page. ("Charset" is short for "character set.") From time to time if you don't specify character encoding your page may be display gibberish.

Heading tags are similar to the headings that you would use in a Word processing document such as Microsoft Windows as shown in this illustration.

AaBbCcI **AaBbC** AaBbCc *AaBbCcI* AaB AaBbCc. AaBbCcD

¶ No Spaci... Heading 1 Heading 2 Heading 4 Title Subtitle Subtle Em...

Styles

Horizontal Rules

Horizontal rules are another way to separate sections of text or content on a Web page to make it look more interesting. The **<hr>** tag places a thin grey horizontal line across the Web browser's window, dividing everything above it and below it. The **<hr>** tag can also be placed anywhere in a document. (The "hr" stands for "horizontal rule.")

Here is an example of how to place horizontal rules in your HTML document:

```
<hr>
<h2> Title </h2>
<hr>
<p> </p>
<hr>
```

To follow along, type the HTML code into your text editor (Sublime Text) or Windows Notepad, save the file as .html file, and then view it in your browser to see the results. Every Web browser has a tendency to display a horizontal rule in a different way. You can see what a basic one usually looks by viewing Figure 4-1.

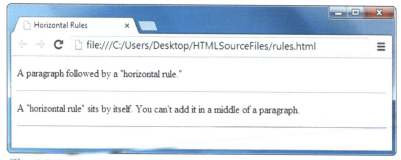

Fig 4-1: Horizontal rules

Indenting Your Code

I recommend getting into the habit of indenting your HTML code. (See the "Headings" HTML document above for an example of indented codes and tags.) Indenting code will save you a lot of time (and pulling your hair out in frustration) when you need to solve problems and/or fix code because it helps you see more clearly where specific code is sitting at a quick glance.

And if you don't indent your HTML code, it also can be difficult seeing where a line of code ends and content begins. Let's take a look at some examples of bad coding practices – and one good practice – to illustrate why indenting your HTML code is so important.

Bad Coding Practice 1: Code on a Single Line

```
<p> Lorem ipsum dolor sit amet, consectetur
adipisicing elit, sed do eiusmod tempor
incididunt. Enim and minum veniam, quis nostrud
exercitation ullamco laboris nisi ut ex ea
commodo consequat. </p>
```

In the example above, see how hard it is to find where code ends and text begins. Most text editors will have a word wrapping capability, but even with this feature turned on, it's hard to find the **</p>** paragraph tag in the HTML code.

Bad Coding Practice 2: Code Not Indented

```
<p> Lorem ipsum dolor sit amet, consectetur
adipisicing elit, sed do eiusmod tempor
incididunt. Enim and minum veniam, quis nostrud
exercitation ullamco laboris nisi ut ex ea
commodo consequat.
</p>
```

In the example above, the HTML paragraph closing tag (</**p**>) *has* been left aligned, but it's still quite difficult to tell code apart from text.

Good Coding Practice: Indenting Your Code

```
<p>
    Lorem ipsum dolor sit amet, consectetur
    adipisicing elit,sed do eiusmod tempor
    incididunt. Enim and minum veniam, nostrud
    exercitation ullamco laboris nisi ut ex ea
    commodo consequat.
</p>
```

In the example above, the HTML code is indented. The paragraph tags <p> ... </p> are placed on a separate line as to distinguish plain text from code. You can see how easy it is to find where the paragraph tag begins and ends.

Here are a few examples of indenting HTML code and text in my favorite code editor Sublime Text 2.

```
C:\Users\Mitesh\Desktop\paragraphs.html - Sublime Text 2 (UNREGISTERED)

File  Edit  Selection  Find  View  Goto  Tools  Project  Preferences  Help

paragraphs.html          x

1   <!doctype html>
2   <html>
3   <head>
4       <meta charset="utf-8" />
5       <title> </title>
6   </head>
7
8   <body>
9       <p>
10          Lorem ipsum dolor sit amet, consectetur adipiscing elit. Morbi
            imperdiet tortor id ligula vulputate volutpat.
11      </p>
12  </body>
13  </html>
14

Line 11, Column 9                              Tab Size: 4         HTML
```

Note: See how the text and contents of the Web page have been indented within the paragraph tags **<p>** | **</p>** and are sitting inside the **<blockquote>** tag. This is known as **nesting**.

Formatting in Your Text Editor

If you're using an HTML editing program instead of a simple text editor such as Windows Notepad or TextEdit for the Mac, you have the ability to automatically indent your code. To do this in Sublime Text 2, select your HTML code then choose Edit > Line > Re-indent to automatically format your code.

Block Quotes

A **<blockquote>** is an HTML element for citing a text quote from a person or a document. This particular tag tells the Web browser that the text sitting inside this element is a quotation. When you use this element, your browser will automatically indent text on the left and the right side.

Create a new document in Sublime Text 2 by selecting File | New. Now type the code exactly as you see here:

```
<p> <b> Albert Einstein: </b> </p>
<blockquote>

    <p> I am enough of an artist to draw freely
        upon my imagination. Imagination is
        more important than knowledge.
        Knowledge is limited. Imagination
        encircles the world.
    </p>

</blockquote>
```

Once you've done this save your file with the name **quote.html** in your folder on your desktop. Preview your page in your Web browser to check your work.

Figure 4-1 shows how this appears in a Web browser.

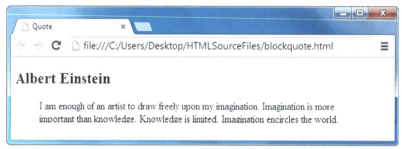

Fig 4-1: A block quote is normally indented from the heading

If a quote is written somewhere else – in a printed magazine, a book, or even on a Web page on the Internet, you can mention where you found the quote. To do this you have to use the **<cite>** element (for citation). A citation will usually format the text in italics. Here is what using the **<cite>** element looks like:

<p>
Your time is limited, so don't waste it living someone else's life. Don't be trapped by dogma – which is living with the results of other people's

thinking. Don't let the noise of others opinions drown out your own inner voice. And most important, have the courage to follow your heart and intuition. **<cite>** – Steve Jobs **</cite>**
</p>

You can also add a URL (Uniform Resource Locater) that will point to the actual source of the quote on the Web by using the <cite> element like this:

<blockquote cite="http:// onstartups.com/tabid/3339/bid/79666/8-Ways-Writing-a-Book-Is-Like-Starting-a-Company.aspx">
    <p>
    If you've wondered why I haven't been blogging it's because I have been writing a book called the ultra light Startup. I wish I had this book when I first started out as an entrepreneur a few years ago. While writing, I realized that creating a book is a very similar process to the process of starting up a small business.
    </p>
</blockquote>

Before going any further, open up the Web page we created earlier called **quote.html** and add the **<cite>** tag to it and then preview your Web page in your browser to check your work.

The **<blockquote>** element will not look any different from other HTML tags we have learnt throughout this book. Remember, HTML markup language is not designed to format text. To do this we have to use style sheets that have been specially created for formatting page elements. (We talk about style sheets in depth in Chapter 7.)

Creating Lists

Lists help you to organize tasks and get things done. Thankfully, HTML also allows you to create lists on your Web page. A list is used to draw attention to short pieces of text on your page. HTML includes a set of special tags for creating three types of lists: unordered lists, ordered lists and definition lists.

- **Unordered lists** are generally known as bulleted lists. A bullet point appears before each item on the list.

- **Ordered lists** are similar to bulleted lists, but each item is sequentially numbered or lettered (as in 1, 2, 3 and 4 or a, b, c and d).

- **Definition lists** are lists of items with a description of each item. For example, pages in a dictionary are definition lists. On a Web page, definition lists are left aligned, and the definitions are usually indented underneath.

In the following sections, you'll learn how to create all three types of lists.

Unordered List

In an unordered (or bulleted) list, items are not sequentially numbered or lettered. Instead, a "bullet" appears before each item. A bulleted list is created by first using the **<ul>** (unordered list) tag and then tagging each item in the list inside a **<li>** (llst item) clemont. Your Web browser will indent each item on the list and draw bullet points before each.

Create a new document in Sublime Text 2 by selecting File |

New. Now type the code exactly as you see here:

```
<!doctype html>
<html>
  <head>
  <title> Lists </title>
  <meta charset="UTF-8" />
  </head>
<body>
  <h1> Lists: To Do </h1>
  <p> These are the tasks I have to complete:
</p>
  <hr>
  <ul>
    <li> Stop magazine subscription </li>
    <li> Empty recycling bins</li>
    <li> Take dog for a walk</li>
  </ul>
</body>
</html>
```

Once you've done this save your file with the name **lists.html** in the HTML folder on your desktop. While typing in the HTML markup tags can be a hassle, it's the best way to learn HTML coding. Don't be worried about making mistakes, as you'll feel a sense of accomplishment when, with practice, you can spot errors and fix them yourself.

Preview your page in your Web browser to check your work. Figure 4-2 shows how this will appear in a Web browser.

If you look carefully at the HTML source code you'll notice that there are no bullet points. These bullet points are automatically added by the Web browser (Figure 4-2).

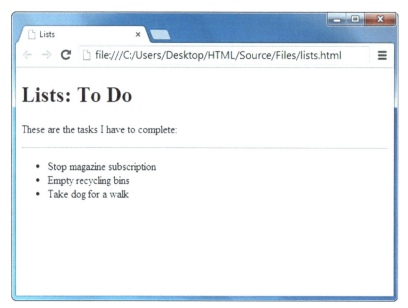

Fig 4-2: Using <ol> and <li> tags to create unordered lists

Ordered List

In an ordered list, you use HTML tags (elements) to specify numbers or letters for each item on your list in order (for example, 1 to 4 or a to d). The Web browser will then automatically display numbers or letters next to each item on the list (similar to the number list feature in Word). A numbered ordered list is created by using the **<ol>** (ordered list) element; inside it you place the **<li>** (list item) element to list each item.

Before going any further, open up the Web page we just created – "lists.html" – in Sublime Text 2 and add the following code to it.

```
<h1> How to boil an egg</h1>
<hr>
<p> <b> A recipe for boiling eggs: </b> <p>
<hr>
<ol>
```

(Cont'd)

```
    <li> Place the egg in a small pan, add a
    pinch of salt and place on high heat. </li>
    <li> When the water is boiling, gently stir
    the egg. </li>
    <li> Reduce heat slightly to keep water
    bubbling and stir the egg once more </li>
    <li> Once cooking time is complete, remove
    egg from pan and serve immediately.</li>
  </ol>
```

Save your file with the name: ordered list.html and then click on the Refresh or Reload button in your Web browser to check your work.

Note that the HTML tag <ol> is the default ordered list tag and will display numbers only on your Web page. To make the ordered list show *letters* instead of numbers, specify **type="A"** for uppercase letters and **type="a"** for lowercase letters in the <ol> element. Here's an example of HTML tags for an ordered list with uppercase letters.

```
<ol type="A">
   <li>Milk</li>
   <li>Toilet paper</li>
   <li>Coffee</li>
</ol>
```

And here's how your Web browser will display the list.

    A. Milk
    B. Toilet paper
    C. Coffee

Definition List

In a definition list each definition item usually has two parts: A list to show the terms being defined, and the definitions indented underneath them. A definition list is created by using the **<dl>** (definition list) element. Then you wrap each item in your list in a **<dt>** (definition term) element, and finally, each definition sits in a **<dd>** (dictionary definition) element.

Open up the Web page we just created – "lists.html" – in Sublime Text 2 and add the following code to it.

```
<h1> Web Glossary </h1>
<hr>
<p> A list of Web Glossary terms. <p>
<hr>

<dl>

    <dt> HTML </dt>
    <dd> HTML (Hypertext Markup Language) is
    the language of the World Wide Web. </dd>
    <dt> WYSIWYG </dt>
    <dd> WYSIWYG (What You See Is What You
    Get). Dragging and dropping layouts in an
    editor as you see fit without worrying
    about any coding. </dd>

    <dt> HTML Page </dt>
    <dd> A document written in HTML. </dd>
</dl>


    <dt> HTML Page </dt>
    <dd> A document written in HTML. </dd>
```

Save your file with the name **definition list.html,** then click on the Refresh or Reload button in your Web browser to check your work. Figure 4-3 shows how this will appear in a browser

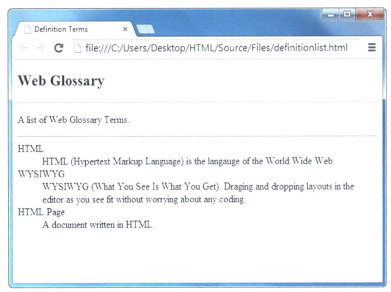

Fig 4-3: shows how a browser will display a definition list

Adding Comments to an HTML file

The beauty of HTML is that you also have the ability to add comments to your code. These are hidden from view so a visitor to your Web site will never find these unless they actually look at your HTML code. These comments or reminders can be notes to yourself or directions to another person who may edit your code at a later date. Normally, comments are hidden and will not be displayed by the Web browser. Comments can only be viewed when you view the source code of the HTML page.

You can create a comment in your HTML document by typing **<!-- to** mark the start of a comment, plus your HTML comment (code) and the list item it refers to, and then typing --> to end your comment. The Web browser will ignore everything sitting between these tags (<!-- | -->) whether it's content or code. I use commenting to hide sections of an HTML page, as I don't have to make any permanent changes to my code. It's a very handy trick to know.

Here is an example of a navigation list that hides one list item (the "Contact Us" item). When you view it in your browser you will only see the first two items.

```
<ul>
<li> <a href="#"> About Us </a> </li>
<li> <a href="#"> Portfolio </a> </li>
<!-- hide code
<li> <a href="#"> Contact Us </a> </li>
-->
</ul>
```

When you want to return the navigation list to its original state, simply remove the HTML comments.

Chapter 5

Linking Pages

You've now grasped the basics of creating single Web pages using HTML. The great thing about HTML is its capability to link to several pages on the Internet. After all, linking is what makes the Web so special. In this chapter we'll look at the HTML code that makes linking possible: the anchor element.

If you're familiar with the Web you may have seen navigation text and graphics that say "click here." These are officially known as **hyperlinks**, and when you click on them they transport you to another part of the Internet.

Adding Links to Other Web Pages

In HTML, you have to use the **<a>** (anchor) tag to create links between pages. When a visitor clicks on a link, a Web browser will load up another page. The link may point to another page on the Web, or to graphics, video, software, email addresses and/or downloadable files. In fact anything you can see through your browser window can be linked to and from an HTML page.

The starting and closing anchor tag looks like this: **<a> | </a>**

To make it into a proper, clickable link for a Web page visitor, you have to enclose the URL of the destination that you want to go to on the Web *inside* the **<a>** start tag and use an **HREF** (hypertext reference) attribute, THEN add the anchor text (in this example, "Click here") that you want the visitor to click on. Finally, close the hyperlink code with the ending anchor tag -- </a>. Your line of code should look like this:

<a href="http://www.google.com"> Click here </a>

Anchor links are by default underlined and displayed in blue as shown in Figure 5-1. However, by using cascading style sheets (CSS), you can change the formatting and style of a hyperlink. We discuss this and CSS in-depth in Chapter 7.

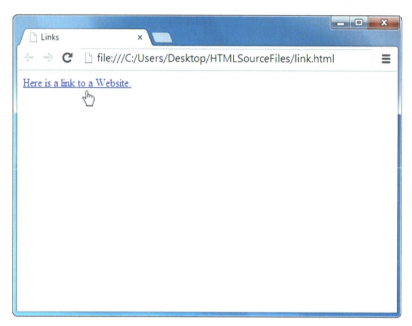

Fig 5-1: A example of an anchor link

Opening a New Window

You can also open a new window in your browser without leaving your original Web page. This is a common trick that all Web developers use as it allows a Web site visitor to click on a link and not leave the original page. It basically opens an external new page in a separate browser window, but your original page is still left intact so that Website visitors don't forget about you.

Create a new document in Sublime Text 2 by selecting File | New. Now type this code exactly as you see here:

```
<!doctype html>
<html>
  <head>
  <title> Linking </title>
  <meta charset="UTF-8" />
  </head>
<body>
  <p> Visit me at <a
href="http://thehappymonk.net" target="_blank">
My Blog </a>  </p>
</body>
</html>
```

Now save your file with the name **links.html** and preview it in your Web browser to check your work. (Depending upon which browser you use, you will see the external Web page in a new tab or in a separate browser window).

The only difference with this specific link is the target element (`target="_blank"`), which tells the browser where to open a linked page. The value **_blank** indicates that the link should open in a new empty browser window.

Adding Links to Sections on the Same Page

HTML also has the capability to link to other sections of your page. To do this you have to specify a name for a section of your page in the anchor tag, then when you click on the name/link you'll be taken to it. If you don't name a section you won't be able to link to it.

Here is a straightforward example of a named anchor:

<a name="Part 1"> Part 1 </a>

The **\<name\>** element simply gives a name to a section of your Web page. So first, you have to create an **anchor link** pointing to that named section like this:

<a href="#Part1"> Part 1 </a>

To create the anchor link you use the **\<a\>** tag and the **HREF** attribute as you normally would when you're creating a link. You then need to add a hash symbol (**#**) and the **anchor name** you are actually linking to. (The hash symbol tells the browser that you are linking to a specific section on the same Web page).

Now create a new document in Sublime Text 2 by selecting File | New. Types in this code exactly as you see here:

```
<!doctype html>
<html>
  <head>
  <title> Linking on a same page</title>
  <meta charset="UTF-8" />
  </head>

<body>
  <ul>
    <li> <a href="#Part1"> Jump to part 1 </a> </li>
    <li> <a href="#Part2"> Jump to part 2 </a> </li>
    <li> <a href="#Part3"> Jump to part 3 </a> </li>
  </ul> <!--end navigation-->
  <hr>

  <a name="Part1"> <h2> Part 1 </h2> </a>
    <p> Text for Part 1 goes in here... </p>
  <hr>

  <a name="Part2"> <h2> Part 2 </h2> </a>
    <p> Text for Part 2 goes in here... </p>
  <hr>
  <a name="Part3"> <h2> Part 3 </h2> </a>
```

(Cont'd)

```
   <p> Text for Part 3 goes in here... </p>
   <hr>
</body>
</html>
```

Mailto Links

A mailto link is a special link that allows Web site visitors to send you email. When you click on a mailto link, your browser will automatically open up your default email program, and then you can begin to craft your message. A blank email addressed to whatever address you've included in the link will open. The link won't automatically send mail. You still have to do that by hitting "send" in your email program.

To create a mailto link, you have to start with **mailto element** followed by a **colon (:)** and then your email address. Here is an example:

<a href="mailto:me@sample.com"> Email me </a>

You can also supply additional text for your email subject line and the body, so that when you click on a mailto link, the message will load up with this information ready to send or edit. Here is another example that includes the subject line:

<a href="mailto:me@sample.com?subject=Hi"> Email me </a>

Here is another example that includes both the subject line and the body of the email message:

<a href="mailto:me@sample.com?subject="Hi&body=I love your site."> Email me </a>

Chapter 6

Adding Graphics

Before the dawn of the Web, the first few pages on the Internet were text only and didn't contain any images. A Web page with just text and no images isn't much fun to look at. The Web can be a very dull place without any graphics, images, videos, ads and animated graphics.

In this chapter you'll learn how to add graphics to your Web pages and how to position and size images. You'll also learn how to use alternate text that will be displayed if a Web browser can't display your graphic images.

The <img> Element

To add images on your Web page, you have to use the **<img>** (image) tag followed by **src** (which stands for **source**) and a URL that links to your image file. For example, here is an **<img>** tag that displays a file named **photo.jpg**:

```
<img src="photo.jpg" />
```

The image tag tells the Web browser to insert an image on your page. The SRC attribute specifies the location of the image file on your computer. You don't have to start and close tags in this particular element. Instead, you have to add the forward slash (/) before the angled bracket at the end of the tag.

Alternate Text

The alternate text (**alt**) attribute will be displayed in your browser if visitors aren't able to see any images on your page.

Here is an example using the **alt** attribute:

<img src="photo.jpg" alt="There is no image, it's just alternate text." />

The **alt** attribute provides a brief description of an image if for any reason a Web site visitor can't see it (for example, because of a slow connection, an error in the **src** attribute, or if the website visitor is using a screen reading program).

Specifying Width and Height of Images

The **<img>** (for "image") element has two more attributes named **width** and **height**. These set the width and the height of an image in your Web page. If you don't specify the width and height of an image, some browsers will wait until all the images are downloaded before you can view the page.

Specifying the width and height of an image can help to speed up the downloading process. The browser will load the Web page much quicker and allow Web site visitors to read content and click on links as the page actually downloads.

Here is an example of a tag with the width and height attributes added:

<img src="photo.jpg" alt="#" width="100" height="200" />

In this HTML code, you have given the image a width of 100 pixels and a height of 200 pixels. You can also use this code to change an existing image and force it to a width and height you want. This is *not* recommended, however, because doing so will increase your file size and lead to longer download times.

Aligning Images and Text

The **<img>** (image) tag also has an additional attribute called **align**, which controls how text and images line up on a page. Here is an example of the **image** tag with the **align** attribute added to it:

<img align="top" src="photo.jpg" alt="#">

The **align="top"** attribute aligns the image to the top edge of the browser window. The **src** attribute links to the location of the image you want to display on your Webpage. Table 6-1 below lists the basic **align** attributes. Note that **align** is an **inline element.** This means that you can't use it as a stand-alone element in the **<body>** section of your HTML document. You have to place it *inside* a block level element. A **block level element** is any group of tags like this:

<p> Here is a paragraph </p>

The **<img>** (**image**) tag is also another inline element that you have to place *inside* block level elements like this:

<p> <img src="photo.jpg" alt="#"> Here is a paragraph </p>

Table 6-1 Values for Align Attribute

Property	Description
"top"	Aligns the image to the top of page
"middle"	Aligns the image to the middle of page
"bottom"	Aligns the image to the bottom of page

Chapter 7

Cascading Style Sheets

In the last chapter you learnt that HTML is limited and that it can't be used to format your documents the way you want it to. If you want your Web pages to look good, you'll have to add style sheets to your bag of tricks.

A style sheet is a document that contains formatting rules. A Web browser will simply read these rules and apply the formatting to your page. Using style sheets allows you to control page elements such as borders, colors, and margins, and to even embed fonts that aren't available locally on your computer.

Style sheets are officially known as CSS (for Cascading Style Sheets). CSS is a separate language with its own syntax, but don't let that frighten you. This language was specifically developed for formatting Web pages. It's so powerful that with a single command you can alter the appearance of a Web page.

You should always put your CSS rules into a separate file instead of embedding them directly into your Web page. The reason we do this is that it separates HTML code from your CSS rules and makes updating code much easier in the long run.

Before the introduction of CSS, Web designers looked for other ways to change the layouts on their Web pages. One such way was using table tags--a separate set of HTML tags that are used to make tables, table headers, table row, and so forth. But table tags were often misused. Instead of adding structure to a page, they were often being used to layout Web pages. And back before CSS, making changes to a large Web site with table tags or other formats was just difficult, time consuming and expensive, because you had to edit each page of a site individually.

CSS was specifically developed to eliminate the difficulties, expense, and time involved in using table tags. Just by editing a single CSS file you can instantly make changes to a large and complex Web site. For example, you can create a CSS rule to format font sizes, and every page on your Web site will then be updated to reflect those specific changes.

In this chapter, you'll learn how to create style sheets and how to attach them to a document – by placing them within the **<head>** section of the Web page, or by linking them to the Web page as a separate file. You'll also learn how to create a style and apply it to your Web page. But before we do that, here's a brief history of the evolution of CSS.

A Brief History of CSS

HTML – Hypertext Markup Language – was never intended to be used to control the appearance of a Web page. It is a language used simply to describe the contents of a page like this:

```
<!doctype html>
<html>
<head>
. . .
</head>
<body>
. . .
</body>
```

</html>

HTML was developed mainly to display text and content in a Web browser – a medium used to disseminate information on the Internet – with little thought given to the layout (or "look") of the page. In fact, it was left up to the Web browsers to decide how a page was displayed.

But as the Web grew in popularity, Web designers started looking for other ways to change the layout of a page, and this lead to the use and misuse of table tags to "design" pages, as we discussed earlier. But table tags weren't intended to be used as layout guides; so while they were effective, they were also inefficient.

To meet this growing Web design need, the two most popular browsers at that time (Netscape Navigator and Internet Explorer) created new HTML tags for this very purpose like the **font** and **color** tags. However designers continued to use table tags to layout Web pages and this system became increasingly popular in the design community. But as the Web grew, maintaining large and more complex Web sites became increasingly difficult. HTML code got longer and more complicated and this led to longer download times.

To solve this problem the World Wide Web consortium (W3C) created CSS (Cascading Style Sheets) by separating Web site content from the presentation format. Web site content refers to the HTML structure of a web page and presentation basically refers to how the Web site content is displayed on the page.

Your First Style Sheet

Now it's time to put it all together and create your first CSS (Cascading Style Sheet).

If you're familiar with Web and have visited many Web sites, you'll know that your browser displays text links in blue and with an underline. (This is the browser's default (automatic) format display for text links.) But what if the blue links are at odds with the general look and feel of your own Web page?

You can build a style sheet rule that will change the text color of the link on your Web page. To do this, you simply have to use a CSS style attribute and declare it within an HTML element. Here is an example:

<a href="#" style:"color: red;"> Click Here </a>

A style attribute is made up of two parts: a property name and a value. Here is the format every attribute follows and how it looks as code:

<style: property; name: value;>

In this example, the property specifies the type of formatting that is applied to your HTML element. Here "color" is the property, which sets the color of the anchor link. The value is the actual name of the color – "red. In another example of a CSS style attribute, the property name might be "font" and the value could be the "size" of font.

This CSS rule is commonly known as a **statement**. A statement is simply a piece of code; here, all it does is specify the style property as **color** and make the anchor link ("Click Here") **red (the color "value")**.

Create a new document in Sublime Text 2 by selecting File | New. Now type this code exactly as you see here:

```
<!doctype html>
<html>
  <head>

  <title> My First Style Sheet </title>

  <meta charset="UTF-8" />
  </head>

<body>

  <p> <a href="#" style="color:red; text-
decoration:none;">
  Click Here </a> </p>

</body>
</html>
```

Once you've done this, save your file with the name **colors.html** in your HTML folder on your desktop. Now preview your file in your Web browser to check your work.

To remove the standard underlined text from your anchor link, use the **text-decoration** attribute and the value **none** (see example above, after **color:red**). The text-decoration is used to set the appearance of text – you can remove underlines, underline standard text, add a line above or through the middle of text and make the text blink.

The text-decoration attribute has the following possible values: underline, line-through, overline, none and blink. Here is an example of code for text decoration that makes the text blink:

text-decoration: blink;

Open up the Web page we've just been working on called colors.html and add the other values to the text-decoration attribute. Preview the file in your Web browser to see how your work is displayed.

```
<p> <a href="#" style="color:red; text-
decoration:blink;">

Click Here </a> </p>
```

Try experimenting yourself by adding the values: **underline, line-through and overline** to the text-decoration attribute and see what happens.

Inline Styles

Inline styles allow you to insert a property name and value of a style sheet right into an HTML tag. But you should try to avoid using this approach if you can. As Inline styles mix formatting with HTML markup, and it becomes difficult to make changes to your Web page: every style on a page must be hunted down in the source code – as you'll soon see.

So here is our earlier example used to format an anchored link:

<a href="#" style="color:red; text-decoration:none;"> Click Here </a>

The rule above removes the default underline of the anchored link and makes the text color red. Inline style may seem much easier to use – it's straightforward, and you can apply it wherever you want on a page. But if you format a page like this it can get quite messy and confusing. You'll soon realize why Web designers tend not to use this technique. Adding inline style to each and every HTML tag on your Web page not only makes the code difficult to read, but it is almost impossible to separate the presentation formatting (style sheets) from the actual HTML. For example, let's consider our earlier example but with several inline style rules added to the tag:

<a href="#" style="color:red; text-decoration:none; border-style: solid; border-color:blue; text-align: left; font-size: 16"> Click Here </a>

See how the anchor tag is already becoming a bit disorderly and chaotic. It's quite difficult to separate content ("Click Here") from the presentation formatting in the example above. So as good practice, HTML markup should always be in a separate, presentation-free document. If you can, try to avoid using inline styles entirely.

The Anatomy of a CSS Rule

A style sheet is made up of rules. A **rule** is a formatting instruction that tells the Web browser to apply specific styles to your Web page.

Here is an example of a CSS rule that sets the color of a **<p>** paragraph element to **red**:

p { color:red;}

The CSS rule is then applied to our <p> paragraph element in the HTML document like this:

<p> Do not go where the path may lead, go instead where there is no path and leave a trail.
</p>

Figure 7-1 shows an example of this paragraph style in action in a standard Web browser.

Fig 7-1: A css rule applied to the paragraph element

If you open up a style sheet to view the code in your browser, you'll see that CSS rules don't have any resemblance to HTML markup. Every CSS rule is basically made up of three things: **selectors**, **properties** and **values**. Ordinarily the property and value is always terminated by a **semicolon(;)**.

Here is the format every CSS rule follows:

Selector {property: value;}

And here is what each part of the CSS rule actually means:

- The **selector** is an HTML element that you want to apply formatting to. For example the (<p>) paragraph tag can be used as a selector. A Web browser will then look for all the common elements In your Web page that match the selector and apply the code within the curly braces to your elements.

- The **property** simply identifies the type of formatting you want to apply to your HTML element. So here you can choose from colors, fonts, sizes and so forth.

- The **value** sets a value for the property. For example, if the property is **color**, then the **value** could be green or light blue.

Selectors, properties and values are essentially the basic building blocks of CSS rules. Once you begin to understand these, you're well on your way to becoming a style sheet guru.

Creating an External Style Sheet

Create a new document in Sublime Text 2 by selecting File | New. Now type this code exactly as you see here:

```
a {
   color:red; text-decoration: none;
}

h1 {
   font-family: arial, sans-serif
}
```

Before you go any farther, save your file with the name **style.css** in your main HTML folder on your desktop. A style sheet can have whatever name you want but must always use the file name extension **.css**. Remember, always save the style sheet in the same folder as your HTML pages, otherwise your page will not display the formatting.

Next, open the file **colors.html** created in the exercise earlier in this chapter. Instead of embedding a style sheet directly into an HTML tag, you will be adding a link to the external **.css** style sheet from within the **<head>** portion of your document.

In the **colors.html** file, simply remove the inline style that was added to the anchor link previously. For comparison purposes, below are the old colors.html file *with* inline style and new colors.html file *without* inline style:

COLORS.HTML FILE WITH INLINE STYLE –

```
<!doctype html>
<html>
 <head>
 <title> My First Style Sheet </title>
 <meta charset="UTF-8" />
 </head>

<body>
 <h1> My First Style Sheet </h1>
 <p> <a href="#" style="color:red; text-decoration:none;">
Click Here </a> </p>

</body>
</html>
```

COLORS.HTML FILE *WITHOUT* INLINE STYLE –

```
<!doctype html>
<html>
    <head>
    <title> My First Style Sheet </title>
    <meta charset="UTF-8" />
    </head>

<body>
    <h1> My First Style Sheet </h1>
    <p> <a href="#"> Click Here </a> </p>
  </body>
</html>
```

Save your file and preview it in your Web browser to check your work. You will see that the formatting rules in the style sheet has not yet been applied to your Web page. This is because we haven't told the browser to point (link) to the style sheet.

To do this you have to add the **<link>** element to the **<head>** portion in your HTML document. The <link> element simply points the browser to the external style sheet and the browser will then apply the style sheet's formatting rules to your page.

Here is the <link> element added to the <head> portion of our page:

```
<!doctype html>
<html>
  <head>
  <title> My First Style Sheet </title>
  <link rel="stylesheet" href="style.css" />
  <meta charset="UTF-8" />
  </head>

<body>
  <h1> My First Style Sheet </h1>
  <p> <a href="#"> Click Here </a> </p>
  </body>
</html>
```

The <link> element has two parts to it. The **rel attribute** simply defines the relationship between the current page and the linked document. In actual fact, you are telling the Web browser it's a style sheet.

The **href** attribute (href stands for **hypertext reference**) points to the actual location of the external style sheet. When you're linking to a style sheet the rel attribute should always be a style sheet.

Save the file and then open it in your Web browser to see

your work. Congratulations! You've just created your first external style sheet.

Create and Organise Folders

A good practice to get into is organizing your images, style sheets, HTML files and JavaScript files into subfolders. JavaScript is a programming language used to add dynamic interactions to a standard HTML page. It allows you to add functionality like the current date and time to your page and make changes to page elements when a web site visitor moves over it. As you begin developing your Web site, you will be adding pictures, files, and snippets of code into your main folder; this collection of data and information will quickly build up, and you may have problems managing and organizing all your information. You may end up with a very large folder containing a mixture of style sheets, pictures, scripts and files. To find a specific file, you will then have to navigate through hundreds of files just to find it. I know that being organized is somewhat dull and uninspiring, but it's very important.

To organize your Web site, you will have to create subfolders in your main folder for each category and type of file. So here's how to do it:

1. First of all, browse to your main folder where you've kept all your HTML related files as you've complete the exercises in this book. (I have named my main folder HTML on my desktop and I've stored all my HTML related files in there.)

2. Open your folder and copy and paste all your HTML related files if you haven't done this yet.

3. To create subfolders within your main folder, right click on your mouse, and then go to New Folder. Now rename this new folder to **images**. This subfolder will mainly be used to hold images that will be used on your Web site.

4. Create another subfolder (New Folder) in your main folder. Rename this folder to **styles** and place all of your style sheets in here.

Most Web sites will tend to grow fairly quickly to over five pages if they are being maintained on a regular basis. By the time you've added a few more pages, a bit of content to explain something in greater depth and some more pictures, it all adds up pretty quickly. I know from experience that you'll be a lot better organized if you do store related HTML files in separate folders.

Now for the tricky part: Because you've reorganized the Web site and moved the external style sheet into a separate folder called **styles**, the style sheet link previously declared in the <head> portion of the Web page will no longer work, because the URL is not pointing to the location of the style sheet since it's been moved.

Before you organized your Web site folder with subfolders, the style sheets were normally referenced like this:

<link rel="stylesheet" href="style.css" />

But here is the link element in the <head> portion of the Web page updated to reflect the new CSS changes:

<link rel="stylesheet" href="css/style.css" />

Here, the style sheet has been placed into a subfolder called **styles**. You then have to tell the Web browser the location of this subfolder on your desktop. The **href** (hypertext reference) tells the browser to look in the **styles** folder and get the file named **styles.css**.

The Need for Divs

Before we go any farther, browse to your Web site folder and open your external CSS file in Sublime Text 2 called style.css. If you've done this you will see the following CSS (Cascading Style Sheet) rules displayed from an earlier exercise that we completed:

```
a {
   color:red; text-decoration: none;
}

h1 {
   font-family: arial, sans-serif
}
```

To add margins around the Web page elements, you will have to use the **margin-left** attribute. To do this, simply type the following code into your style sheet document like this:

```
a {
   color:red; text-decoration: none;
   margin-left: 50px;
}

h1 {
   font-family: arial, sans-serif;
   margin-left: 50px;
}
```

Once you've done this save your file and check your work in your Web browser. Don't forget to add the semicolon (;) at the end of the CSS rules! (Occasionally I forget to do this, and then wonder why my page won't work in my browser.)

The **px in the above code** stands for **pixels**, a unit of measurement on a computer monitor that is commonly known as a dot. Computer monitors display pictures by dividing the screen into millions of pixels, arranged in rows and columns. The pixels are so close that it appears like they are connected together. For example, an image resolution on your computer monitor of 1024 x 768 means that your monitor displays images 1,024 pixels wide and 768 pixels high.

Combining Selectors

So far you've seen style sheet rules being applied to specific HTML elements on your Web page. But CSS (Cascading Style Sheets) is flexible enough to allow you to group CSS selectors and HTML tags together. For example, when modifying a Web page, you may sometimes want to modify just the paragraph and the heading tag, but don't want to type in the formatting rules every time for each element on your page. Let's look at how we can do that.

In the earlier exercise, margin-left attribute was inserted to add some margins around the elements on the Web page. Now open up the style sheet we created earlier called **style.css** and type in this code exactly as you see it here:

```
h1, p {

  margin-left: 50px;
```

Once you've done this, save your file and check your work in your Web browser to make sure the new code is functioning and displaying properly. This piece of code saves you from repeatedly typing the margin-left attribute every time you want to apply it to a paragraph and a heading element on your Web page. Note that the CSS selectors are always separated by a comma. In our example above, for instance, the selectors are "h1" (for heading 1) and "p" (for paragraph) separated by a comma.

When you group CSS selectors and HTML tags, and your Web browser begins processing your HTML document, it will "read" the <link> element pointing to your external style sheet declared in the <head> portion of the page. The browser will then read this rule in the style sheet, which targets all the <h1> and <p> tags in the Web page, and apply the margin-left formatting to them.

The beauty of CSS is that you have the convenience of formatting many HTML elements at once. In the example above, formatting and grouping CSS and HTML code together can produce long lines of code. For example, if you want to add another element to your page, but don't want to apply the same formatting rules to it and want to avoid long lines of code, what do you do?

The <div> Element

A powerful way to apply style sheet formatting to several elements on your Web page is by using the **<div> element**. The div element is used to group one or more elements on a Web page together. You can think of it as a container that you place some things in and "take" wherever you want. Here is a short example:

```
<div>
    <h1> My Website </h1>
    <p>...</p>
    <p>...</p>
    <p>...</p>
</div>
```

The div element is normally used to divide up sections of a

page. It also breaks up your page and adds a clear logical structure to it as well. But it can also be used to great effect when combined with CSS as we'll soon see.

In an earlier exercise, we applied a margin-left attribute to one or more of the page elements on our Web page. Instead of repeatedly typing out this attribute every time we want to use it, you can use the <div> element and format it at once by applying a CSS rule to it.

Let's get started. Create a new document in Sublime Text 2 by selecting File | New. Now type the code exactly as you see here:

```
<!doctype html>
<html>
  <head>
  <title> My First Style Sheet </title>
  <link rel="stylesheet" href="style.css" />
  <meta charset="UTF-8" />
  </head>

<body>
  <div>
      <h1> My First Website </h1>
      <p> <a href="#"> Learn more about me </a>
</p>
      <img src="#" alt="A brief description
about me">
  </div>
</body>
</html>
```

When you're done, save the file with whatever name you want (I've named my file **div.html**) and open it in your Web browser to make sure that it is displaying correctly.

Next, open the file **style.css** in your code editor, and then add the following code to it:

```
div {
  width: 500px;
  margin-left: 50px;
  background: red;
  text-align: center;
}
```

Here's what this code means and what it is doing. We're telling the browser to look for the **<div> element** on the Web page named div.html and apply those formatting rules (see just above) to it. So, the **width property** specifies the width of the container, the **margin-left property** specifies a space of 50px around the element and the **background property** specifies the color of the element; here we've told the browser to make the background a red color. The **text-align property** basically centers the alignment of text within our actual container.

Note: The <div> element is a flexible and versatile all-purpose container. In fact, you can actually use it create snazzy layouts of your page, columns of text, navigation bars and much more. You also have the ability to target <div> elements separately and apply formatting rules to them.

Class and ID Selectors

A **class selector** allows you to target a group of elements on your page by giving them a **class name**. Then you have to tell your Web browser to apply the formatting styles to all those elements that carry that particular class name in the body of your HTML document. Class names are normally preceded with a **period (.)** in the selector.

For example, let's say that you want to change the height and the width of a div element on your page as you might want to include more content and images on your home page. To do this you would simply type the following code into your external style sheet:

```
.content {
    width: 832px;
    height: 370px;
}
```

Once you've done this you will need to add the class name to your HTML elements so that the browser will apply formatting rules to those elements that carry that class name (.content):

```
<div class="content">
<h2> </h2>
<p> . . . </p>
</div>
```

An **ID selector** is somewhat similar to a class selector, but it only allows you to format a single element on your page. To do this, first you will have to pick a descriptive name for your id selector and then, instead of using a **period** before the name, you use a **hash symbol** (#) in the id selector – like this:

```
#about {
display: block;
height: 133px;
width: 340px;
}
```

At this point, you may be wondering what the real difference is between a class selector and an id selector because they seem exactly the same? An id selector can only be applied *once* to an HTML element on a page – meaning you can't reuse it again and again. On the other hand, a class selector can be used as *many* times as you want without any limit.

So now let's practice a couple of ways to format element in

a HTML document using an internal style sheet. Go ahead and launch Sublime Text 2 and create a new file (File | New). Now simply type in the following code exactly as you see it:

```
<html>
  <head>
  <title> </title>
    <meta charset="UTF-8" />
  </head>

<body>
   <ul>
      <li> This </li>
      <li> is </li>
      <li> a </li>
      <li> list </li>
   </ul>
</body>
</html>
```

Save your file with the name **practicelist.html** in your HTML main folder, and check that it is displaying in your Web browser by clicking the REFRESH or RELOAD button.

How do you think you would format the third item in the above list to display it in red? The answer? You would embed an internal style sheet right into the <head> portion of your Web page. While you've been cautioned earlier to avoid using inline styles as a general rule (it's just bad practice and can yield monstrous coding results), sometimes you may use an internal style sheet when you want to send someone a demo of a working Web page – for example, by email – and you don't want to send any extra files as it increases your email file size.

So go back to the file you created earlier in Sublime Text 2 and change it so that it uses an internal style sheet. To do that, add the <style> element inside the <head> section of your web page as shown below:

```
<html>
<head>
<title> </title>
<meta charset="UTF-8" />
</head>
    <style>
    body { background: red; }
    </style>
  </head>

<body>
   <ul>
      <li> This </li>
      <li> is </li>
      <li> a </li>
      <li> list </li>
   </ul>
</body>
</html>
```

Now that we've successfully embedded the style sheet in the <head> section of the document, let's save it and open up the Web page in your browser. You should see a page that looks like the one in figure 7-2. If your page doesn't display correctly, check your HTML file to make sure that you are not missing any angled brackets or a slash at the end of a closing tag as it's so easy to miss.

Fig 7-2: A css rule applied to the paragraph element

Let's have a look again at the embedded style sheet we've just placed inside the HTML document above. Note that the style element must always be contained within a pair of **curly braces** and be terminated by a semicolon (**;**) at the end of the declaration. The **background property** simply sets the background color of the *page* to red.

But . . . to get back to our exercise: How would you select only the *third* item in the list and give it a red color? The answer lies with the **style element** you've just learnt about. Try playing around with that element to see if you can reconfigure it to display the third list item in red. Then check out the solution below.

Go back to the HTML document you just created earlier in Sublime Text 2 and change the style sheet by adding the rule **{ color: red; }** to the **<head>** section of the page, as shown here:

```
<html>
  <head>
  <title> </title>
    <meta charset="UTF-8" />
    <style>
    li { color: red; }
    </style>
  </head>

<body>
   <ul>
     <li> This </li>
     <li> is </li>
     <li> a </li>
     <li> list </li>
   </ul>
</body>
</html>
```

When you are done, save the file and then open it up in your Web browser to check your work. You should see *all* the list items on the Web page in a red color. But remember, you want to select and target only the *third* item on the list and give it a red color.

So, go back to the previously saved HTML file you were working on a moment ago and go to the code for the four list items. Now you simply need to add an HTML **id selector code** that targets the third element in the list, as shown below (the id selector code is in boldface):

```
<ul>
   <li> This </li>
   <li> is </li>
   <li class="highlight"> a </li>
   <li> list </li>
</ul>
```

Note that the id selector has been given a descriptive name for easier reference (I have called it "highlight"). But remember what we discussed earlier: a specific id can only be applied *once* to an HTML element and can't be used again.

Once you've chosen a descriptive name for the id selector, you will need to change the style sheet in the <head> section of the page like this:

```
<style>
#highlight {
   color: red;
}
</style>
```

Save your file and then click the REFRESH or RELOAD button in your Web browser to view the changes you've just made. Your Web browser will read this page and find the hash (#) symbol, which basically tells it to find the CSS rule in the body of the document and apply the color red to the HTML list element. A hash (#) symbol simply tells the browser that a specific id selector has been targeted.

Let's get a little fancier now and use a class selector to target our list item. To add a class selector to your code, simply change the markup in your HTML document for the third list item as shown below:

```
<ul>
   <li> This </li>
   <li> is </li>
   <li class="highlight"> a </li>
   <li> list </li>
</ul>
```

As we've already discussed earlier in this chapter, a class selector is always preceded by a period (.) followed by a descriptive class name. Now simply go ahead change the style sheet in the <head> section of the HTML document to read like this (note the period (.) before "highlight"):

```
<style>
.highlight {
   color: purple;
}
</style>
```

Save your work, and open the file in your Web browser to view it. As we discussed earlier, a class selector can be used as many times as you want. You can target many elements on a page by giving them all the same class name. Then your browser will apply formatting to all the elements that carry that class name in your document.

Floating

On an HTML page, elements are stacked upon one another (similar to blocks), and content within the page flows from the top of the browser window to the bottom. The order in which your page elements are displayed is the same order as in which they appear in your HTML source code. When you use CSS layout properties, however, you can break selected elements out of the flow of a document and rearrange them on a page as you wish.

Float is a basic CSS layout tag. You can take a small portion of quoted text and float it to the left or right of the page, allowing the surrounding text to be wrapped around it. To get a clearer idea of this, look at a photograph or graphic design in a print magazine. It is common to see an image set to the left or right of the page with the text wrapped beautifully around it. This is commonly known as text wrapping, and most word processing programs include this feature.

The following illustration shows an example of a float (text wrapping) layout in a print magazine.

If you're familiar with page layout programs, you'll know that whenever you want to add text to your document, a box is normally created to hold the text. Text boxes can be told to apply text wrapping or ignore wrapping. Ignoring text wrapping will allow the text to flow over the image as if it wasn't there.

Floats work in a similar way and can be used to create entire Web site layouts, navigation elements and table like elements without the use of tables. It's exciting to experiment with floats. Let's try it.

Start a new document in Sublime Text 2 and type in the following code:

```
<html>
  <head>
  <title> </title>
    <meta charset="UTF-8" />
    <link rel="stylesheet"href="css/style1.css>
  </head>

<body>
   <div class="wrap">
   <h1> My Second Website </h1>
   <div id="content">
   <h2> Main Content Heading </h2>
     <p> This is my blog </p>
   </div>

   <aside>
   <h2> Sidebar </h2>
   <ul>
     <li> <a href="#"> Home </a> </li>
     <li> <a href="#"> About </a> </li>
     <li> <a href="#"> Contact </a> </li>
   </ul>
   </aside>
   </div>

</body>
</html>
```

Now save your file with the name **float.html** in your HTML folder. Then click on the REFRESH or RELOAD button in your browser to check your work.

First, notice that a new tag – **<aside>** – has been used in the code you just entered. The **<aside> element** is a fairly new HTML5 tag. All it does is signify a section of the page that is separate from the main content. For example, you can use the <aside> tag to create a sidebar next to a main article with related links and ads.

Next, using style sheets we'll be adding the CSS float property to position a sidebar to the right or left of the page. Open up a new document in Sublime Text 2 by selecting File | New. Then type this code into your code editor (new page):

```css
.wrap {
  width: 600px;
  margin: auto;
}

.content, aside {
  height: 600px;
}

.content {
  background: red;
  float: left;
  width: 450px;
}

aside {
  background: brown;
  float: left;
  padding-left: 0px;
}

aside ul {
  list-style: none;
  padding-left: 0px;
}
```

You will note that this style sheet includes class selectors. The first rule sets the width of the div element named **wrap** in the <body> of the HTML document, and the margin attribute lets the browser decide how much space it can apply around the div element.

The second rule simply sets the height of the div element named **content** and the **<aside>** tag. In the third one, a **background color** is used to single out elements. The **float** property generates a box that is floated to the left of the page and the content flows around it. The **padding** property defines the space between the outside edge of the element and the content that is sitting inside it. The **list-style** property simply gets rid of the bullet points in the sidebar.

Now save your work and take a look at it in your Web browser. It should look like figure 7-3 on this page. If it doesn't, simply go back and recheck your HTML markup and CSS code.

Fig 7-3: The float property

Navigation Lists

Back in Chapter 5, Linking Pages, I showed you how to link to other pages on the Web using the **<a> anchor tag**. If you're familiar with the Web, I'm sure that you've come across navigation menus and links that take you from one section of a Web site to another. After all, an easy-to-use navigation menu is a must for any Web site on the Internet these days.

Normally a navigation menu is made up from a list of links using the **<ul>** and **<li>** elements. In this exercise you will build a navigation menu from a standard HTML list and then format it using a style sheet.

First, let's begin this exercise by creating a new HTML document in your code editor and typing in the following code:

```
<html>
  <head>
    <meta charset="UTF-8" />
    <link rel="stylesheet"
href="css/style2.css>
  </head>

<body>
    <ul>
      <li> <a href="#"> Home </a> </li>
      <li> <a href="#"> About </a> </li>
      <li> <a href="#"> Portfolio </a> </li>
      <li> <a href="#"> Contact </a> </li>
    </ul>
</body>
</html>
```

Save your file with whatever name you want, and then view it in your browser. It's important to always give your file a good descriptive name so that you can find it when you go back to it at a later date. (Here I have saved my file as navigation list.html in my HTML folder.)

By now you should be familiar with creating external style sheets. (If you aren't, I would suggest that you revisit the earlier sections in this chapter to ensure you understand this very important topic.)

To start building your navigation file, create a new document in Sublime Text 2 and call it **style2.css**. Add these CSS rules to it:

```
body {
   font-family: arial, sans-serif;
}

li {
   display: inline;
}
```

The first rule (font-family) is telling the Web browser to pick a generic font that is available on your computer. Sans-serif is a common font that is found on almost every computer these days, including Mac OS, Unix, Linux and Windows. The **font-family attribute** simply specifies the font (arial) used in the main body of the document.

To be on the safe side, whenever you use the font-family attribute you should always end it with a generic font (sans-serif in our example), so that if a specific font is not available on your computer the browser will pick a second font in the sans-serif family.

The second rule (display) targets the listed items. As you learned earlier, a listed item is displayed as a bulleted list in HTML. The **display property** makes the list items line up next to one another instead of starting on a new line.

Save your work and take a look at it in your browser.

Now that all the listed items are on one line, we can remove the underline effect that is applied by default to the **<a> anchor tag**. To do this, go back to the file called **style2.css** and add these rules to it:

```
ul a {
  text-decoration: none;
}
```

Now save your work and take a look at it in your Web browser. You will see that the HTML listed elements are tightly crowded together. To add some space between the elements, add the following rule to the style sheet:

```
li {
  display: inline;
  padding-right: 10px;
}

ul a {
  text-decoration: none;
}
```

Again, save your work and view it in your browser. First, you'll notice that the listed navigation elements have a bit more room between them now. Second, you'll see that when a mouse pointer hovers over a navigation link it changes to a hand symbol – but that symbol is not very clear.

To make the navigation links more noticeable, simply add the following CSS rule in the style sheet:

```
ul a {
  text-decoration: none;
}
ul a: hover {
  text-decoration: underline;
}
```

In this exercise, we've applied a new style to the **hover** state using a new selector called a **pseudo class**. A pseudo class sounds more complicated than it actually is, but you can think of it as a specific effect that is applied to navigation links that have or have not been "clicked" on. There are four main pseudo classes that apply a specific style to an anchor link:

a: link Applies a style to a unvisited link.

a: visited Applies a style to a link that has already been clicked on.

a: hover Applies a style to a link when a mouse pointer is hovering over it.

a: active Applies a style to a link when a mouse button is pressed on the link.

In our example the hover state is linked to the anchor tag, so when a user moves over the link the underline effect is applied to all of the links.

Once you've applied the hover style, save your work and take a look at it in your browser. This navigation menu seems a little boring, doesn't it? Let's add a few finishing touches and some style to the navigation menu. To do this, go back to your navigation HTML document and add the following code:

```
<html>
  <head>
    <meta charset="UTF-8" />
    <link rel="stylesheet"
href="css/style2.css>
  </head>
<body>
  <ul id="nav">
    <li> <a href="#"> Home </a> </li>
    <li> <a href="#"> Services </a> </li>
    <li> <a href="#"> Portfolio </a> </li>
```

(Cont'd)

```
    <li> <a href="#"> About </a> </li>
    <li> <a href="#"> Contact </a> </li>
  </ul>
</body>
</html>
```

The **id attribute** gives the HTML list a unique identifier name so that we can link to it directly in our style sheet. Here I have named it **nav**, short for navigation. Now open up the **style2.css** file in your code editor and make the following changes to it so your style sheet markup now looks like this:

```
ul#nav {
  margin: 0px;
  padding: 0px;
  list-style-type: none;
}

ul#nav li {
  display: inline;
}

ul#nav li a {
  padding: 5px 20px;
  margin: 1px; 0px;
  background-color: #1ea8ce;
  text-decoration: none;
  color: white;
  font-weight: bold;

  border-left: solid 1px #198cac;
  border-right: solid 1px #2db1dc;
  border-top: solid 1px #79cfe8;
  border-bottom: solid 1px #0381a9; }

ul#nav li a:hover {
  background-color: #1c96b9;
  color: #fff; }
```

Save your file and click on the REFRESH or RELOAD button in your Web browser to view the changes you've just made. You can see an example of this in figure 7-4

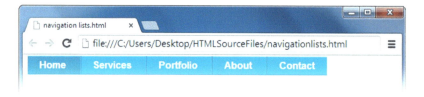

Fig 7-4: The navigation list displayed in a browser

Image Replacement

The **image replacement** technique replaces text (normally a heading tag) on a Web page with an image specified in an external style sheet. The text element is still present in the source code but it is not displayed in the browser as it is hidden from view by CSS (Cascading Style Sheets) magic. The major advantage of this is that your HTML document is accessible to search engines and screen readers. For example, if you wanted to add a logo to your page, you'd add it to the heading tag. But instead of displaying text, you will want to display your logo. Let's do that.

Launch Sublime Text 2 and create a new document by selecting File | New. Add the following code:

```
<head> ... </head>
<body>

<h1> Image Replacement </h1>

</body>
</html>
```

Save your file as **Image Replacement.html** and view it in your Web browser. Now, create a new style sheet in your text editor and add the following rule to it:

```
h1 {
  background: url(..img/logo.jpg) no-repeat;
  text-indent: -9999999px;
}
```

Here I have used an image of a logo that was created in Adobe Photoshop, but you can do a quick search for images on Google and find a suitable image for this exercise on the Web. The **background property** points to the location of the file on the hard drive. Because the file is located in the images folder, you have to go up one level. To do this you have to use this sequence **../** (two periods followed by a slash). To prevent the image from repeating, you use the **no-repeat property**. The **text-indent** simply pushes the text off the screen by using an extremely large negative number that you won't see displayed in your browser.

Forms

Nowadays it's difficult to go on the Web without coming across some sort of form. A form allows a Web site visitor to comment on a recent blog post, add images to a post on a forum, register to receive new email updates or order a product online from Amazon.com. Here we will discuss how to create such forms and use them on your Web site.

An HTML form may contain input fields like text fields, check boxes, radio buttons, text areas, text buttons, drop-down menus and label elements. These elements (collectively known as form controls) are used to collect information from a user. Forms can also contain text and other elements. Figure 7-5 shows an HTML form displayed in a web browser.

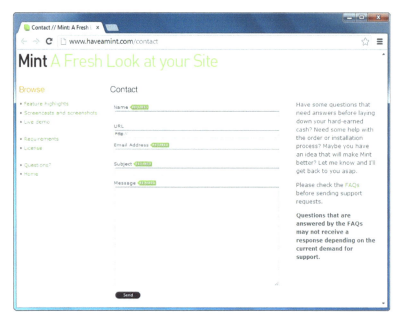

Fig 7-5: A HTML form

Open your code editor, create a new file and type in all the HTML tags as needed to create a basic HTML page like this:

```html
<html>
  <head>
    <meta charset="UTF-8" />
  </head>

<body>

</body>

</html>
```

Save your file as **forms.html** in your HTML folder on your desktop. To create a basic form you have to use the **<form>** element. You can then mix and match input elements with standard HTML markup. As you may have guessed, a form begins with an opening and a closing tag as shown in the following example:

```
<form>
  . . .
</form>
```

A **form element** is basically a container that holds all the elements of a form. Inside it you can place paragraphs of text, graphical form components like buttons, text boxes, lists and so on. All of this is used to capture information that a Web site visitor might enter into the form. I think the best way to learn about forms is to look at some other examples of form online and then give it a try yourself.

Let's go back to **forms.html** and add the following elements to the Web page:

```
<form action="" method="post">
<input/>
</form>
```

As we've previously discussed, the form **element** is a container. HTML takes everything placed inside it as part of the form. The **action property** simply tells the browser where to send the information once it has been submitted. Lastly, the method specifies how to send this information across the Web to the server. There are two methods for sending this data across to the server: **POST** or **GET**. The POST method sends the data separately to the server containing encryption followed then by the data. This is the best method for sending data such as credit card and personal details across the Web. The GET method simply attaches the form details onto the URL, which is then sent to the server.

To get users to enter data on your form, you have to use the **<input>** elements to do this. In fact, you can use this element as many times as you want to describe buttons, text boxes, text fields, text areas, check boxes and so forth. Now let's go back to the HTML document you've got open and add the following code to it:

```
<form action="" method="post">

<input type="submit" value="send"/>

</form>
```

Here we've added a submit button to the HTML form. The type attributes creates a submit button that lets a user submit information that has been entered onto a form. The value lets you define what text appears on the button when a form is displayed. A descriptive name has been given to the button to let users know what it does when you click it.

Whenever you create input elements on an HTML form, you should always include descriptive text that makes it easy for your users to understand what type of information you want them to enter. To create a descriptive text for a text box you have to use a **label element** as shown here:

```
<form action="" method="post">

<label> Enter Your Name: </label>
<input>
<input type="submit" value="send"/>

</form>
```

Save your work and then hit the REFRESH or RELOAD button in your browser to take a look at it. A descriptive text telling the user what to do will be displayed. Now you should see something like the page shown in figure 7-6.

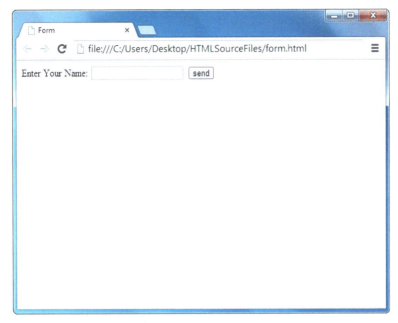

Fig 7-6: A basic HTML form

Now that we've done this it seems like the form is missing something. If you guessed a **text area** you're absolutely correct. Text area is a part of the form where a user can type in information into a field. To create a text area, simply add the following code to the file forms.html:

```
<form action="" method="post">

<label> Enter Your Name: </label>
<input id="name">

<label> Comments </label>
<textarea id="comment"> </textarea>
<input type="submit" value="send"/>

</form>
```

Notice that we've given each input element a unique name so that we can link to it later in a style sheet. Once you've done this, save your work and open it up in your browser to view it. So far, the HTML form looks pretty boring doesn't it? Now let's go ahead and add some style to it using some CSS.

Open up the file **forms.html** in your code editor, and make the following changes:

```
html>
  <head>
    <meta charset="UTF-8" />
    <title> Forms </title>
  </head>

<body>

<div id="text-wrap">
  <h1> Contact Me </h1> </br>

  <p> If you are trying to contact me. PLEASE
DON'T USE
  THIS FORM. This is an example to demonstrate
and it's
  been styled with CSS (Cascading Style
Sheets).
  </p>

  <div id="contact-form">
      <form action="" method="">
          <label> Name: </label>
          <input id="name">
          <label> Email: </label>
          <input id="email">
          <label> Message: </label>
          <textarea id="message"> </textarea>

          <input type="submit" value="send"
class="submit-
              button">
      </form>
  </div>
</div>

</body>
</html>
```

Doesn't that HTML code look quite impressive? Congratulations! You've learnt a lot and got the fundamentals under your belt, but to be really good you have to keep practicing by creating pages and learning from your own mistakes. After making these changes, save the file and view it in your browser by hitting refresh or reload button to view the changes you've just made.

Now, let's add some style to the form. Create a new style sheet named **style3.css** in your code editor and add the following CSS rules to it:

```css
body {
  background-color: #56636f;
  font-family: Helvetica, sans-serif;
}

p {
  font-size: 15px;
  margin-bottom: 10px;
}

#text-area {
  width: 600px;
  height: 430px;
  padding: 20px 50px 20px 50px;
  margin: 20px auto;
  background-color: white;
}

#contact-form {
  width: 580px;
  margin-top: 20px auto;
  float: left;
}
```

Before we go any farther, look at the **body selector**. We've applied a solid background color to the body of the HTML page. In the font-family property we have chosen to use the Helvetica font, meaning every text element displayed on the page will be set to Helvetica. Failing that, the default font will be whichever sans-serif font is currently available on your computer. We have also targeted the **div container** by using an **id selector** called "#text-area" and specified the width and height of the container, to create a rectangular shape and fill it with a solid white color. We've also added some padding to clear an area inside the element. The top margin has been set to 20px and the rest of it is calculated by the browser automatically.

For the contact form we've created a **div element**, called it "contact-form" and targeted it using an **id selector** by using a prefix hash (#). Here, all the form elements are placed inside it. A width of 580px has been specified for the div container and it has been floated to the left of the page. The margin-top property is used to position the contact-form element towards the middle of the page.

Now let's go back to the style sheet **style3.css** and add the following CSS rules to it as shown here:

```
#contact-form textarea {
   height: 100px;
   width: 464px;
   border: 1.5px groove #ccc;
}

#contact-form input {
   width: 464px;
   padding 5px;
   font-family: Helvetica, sans-serif;
   margin: 0 0 10 0;
   border 1.5px groove #ccc;
   font-size 1.2em;
}
```

Looking at the **id selector** "contact-form text area," we've simply specified the height and the width of the text area component. The border property sets the color, the style and the size of the border. In this instance, the groove defines a 3D grooved border around the element and the color has been set to a gray.

The **id selector** "contact-form input" simply specifies the width of the input boxes on the HTML form. The **padding property** clears a space of 5px inside the input element and the actual content you'll enter into the box. To shorten the code, the margin property has been written in a shorthand format. Here we've applied 10px to the bottom margin. By default, CSS includes a shorthand notation format, so instead of retyping **margin-top**, **margin-right**, **margin-bottom** and **left-margin** onto a new line every single time, you can specify all the margin properties on a single line. Looking at the font-size property, what do you think it does? If you guessed that it sets the font size, you're correct. The **em** is basically a unit of size and now we'll just leave it there and move on to the other portion of this exercise.

Let's go back to the style sheet, **style3.css** in your favorite code editor or Sublime Text 2 – if it isn't already open. Now continue to add the following CSS rules to the style sheet as shown here:

```
#contact-form .submit-button {
margin-top: 15px;
width: 100px;
float: right;
}

label {
float: left;
```

(Cont'd)

```
text-align: right;
margin-right: 15px;
width: 100px;
padding-top: 5px;
font-size: 15px;
}
```

After making these changes, save the file and go back to your Web browser. Click on the REFRESH or RELOAD button to view the changes you've just made. Remember that we created a div container in our original HTML document and placed all the form components inside it. The submit button is given a class name, "submit-button," and then we tell the browser to apply formatting to the button placed inside the div container.

Similarly, I have changed the appearance of the label element in the HTML document by using a CSS selector to target it and apply formatting to it. Here the **label** element containing descriptive text has been floated to the left. The text in each label has been right aligned using the text-align property. Then a margin of 15px has been applied to the right to line up the form elements. The padding property sets the space between the edges of the element and the text inside it. Finally, as the last line indicates, the font has been set to a large size (15px).

Relative and Absolute Positioning

By now, you probably know that CSS provides several methods to position and move elements around on a page. An HTML element can be positioned relative to the normal flow of the document, or it can be completely removed from the flow of the document and be placed wherever you want on a Web page.

Let's create a basic HTML document in your code editor

(select File | New). Next, add the following code as I've shown here:

```
<head> ... </head>
<body>

<div class="box">

</div>

</body>
</html>
```

Once you've typed this in, save your work as a file called **position.html** in your HTML folder on your desktop. Here we've created a standard div element in your document and given it a descriptive class name. Feel free to name it whatever you want at this point.

Create a new empty document in your code editor, save it as a file called **style4.css** and type in the following code as shown here:

```
.box {
width: 200px;
height: 200px;
margin: auto;
background: red;
}
```

In this CSS selector, a width and height of 200 pixels has been applied to the div element named "box" on the page. Next, the margin property has been set to **auto**; it simply lets the browser decide how much spacing to add around the element. The **background property** is used to set the color of the div element to red. This is a common trick used by many Web developers to highlight important areas of a Web page. On the other hand, if the background color is not applied, you won't be able see the div element when you view it in your

Web browser. Feel free to experiment by changing the width and height of the .box property in your CSS file.

To view the changes in your Web browser add the following code in the **<head>** section of the HTML document like this:

```
<head>
<link rel="stylesheet" href="css/style4.css">
</head>
```

Be sure to save your work, then click on the REFRESH or RELOAD button in your Web browser to view it. Now let's go back to the **position.html** file and add the following changes to it as shown here:

```
<head> .... </head>
<body>

<div class="box">
<blockquote> When a machine malfunctions you do
not take it personally or grow despondent. It
is in fact a blessing in disguise. Such
malfunctions show you inherent flows and
means of improvement. You simply keep tinkering
until you get it right. The same should apply
to an entrepreneurial venture until you get it
right. <em> Mistakes and failures are precisely
your means of education </em> They tell you
about your own inadequacies.
</blockquote>
<cite> &mdash; Robert Greene, Mastery </cite>
</div>

</body>
</html>
```

Save your work (File | Save) and then click on the REFRESH or RELOAD button in your browser to view it. You can see an example of this in figure 7-7.

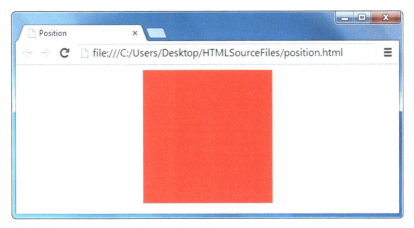

Fig 7-7: A box created using the div property

Open **style.4css** in your code editor and add the following CSS rules into your style sheet:

```
box {
width: 800px;
border: 2px solid #ccc;
padding: 15px;
background-color: #efeecb;
}

body{
font-size: 16px;
font-family: arial, sans-serif;
}

blockquote {
font-family: georgia, serif;
width: 600px;
font-size: 18px;
font-style: italic;
line-height: 1.50
}
```

Next, save the CSS document, and then view your Web page in your browser by clicking on the REFRESH or RELOAD button. As we discussed earlier, relative positioning moves an element relative to its original spot in the normal flow of the document. But then the original spot the element occupied is still preserved and continues to influence the surrounding content.

Sound confusing? Well, there is no better way to understand relative positioning than by seeing it in action. To do this, open up your **style4.css** file and add the following small change to it as shown here:

```
em {
position: relative;
top: 10px;
left: 20px;
background-color: purple;
}
```

Save your file and then click on the REFRESH or RELOAD button in your Web browser to view it. You can see an example of this in figure 7-8.

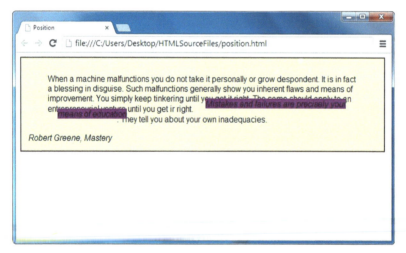

Fig 7-8: Element positioned using relative method

Here an **<em>** element has been set to **relative** positioning using the CSS position property. The **top offset** property moves the element down 10 pixels from its original position, and the **left offset** property moves it 20 pixels to the right. So if you want to move an element to the left, you have to specify the **right offset** property. Normally, the offset property moves an element away from the specified edge of the HTML element.

If you preview the Web page in your browser, you will see there is an empty space where the original element would have been had we not moved it using the position property. You also can see that though we have moved the emphasized text, this empty space seems to influence the surrounding content. Because it is a positioned element, it can also overlap other elements on the page.

Now that you've seen how relative positioning works, let's go back and open the file **position.html** in your code editor. Change the relative positioning value in your file to **absolute** as shown here:

```
em{
position:absolute;
top:40px;
left:60px;
background-color:purple;
}
```

Save your changes and then view your file in your Web browser. You can see an example of this in figure 7-9.

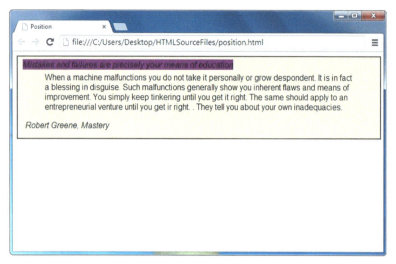

Fig 7-9: Element positioned using absolute method

If you viewed the page in your browser you will see that the absolute positioning method is a little different. It is more flexible for placing elements on a Web page than using relative positioning. Here, the emphasized text has simply been taken out of the flow of the document and placed wherever you want on the Web page. The empty space that was occupied by the **<em>** element is now closed up, and the element overlaps the surrounding text. But unlike relative positioning it has no influence over the surrounding content.

Conclusion

We've covered a lot in this chapter! Congratulations, first give yourself a well-deserved pat on the back for getting this far. This isn't just another Web Design book. It's special, it really is. I set out to create a book that I'd want by my side as I learnt HTML and CSS when I was beginner. Although I haven't taught you everything about HTML and CSS, I do hope that it gives you a good understanding of the things that are possible with it.

Further Reading

If you are eager to learn more about HTML and CSS, the following resources are a good starting point for further exploration of Web design and development. I personally recommend these resources to gain a better understanding of HTML and CSS and to improve your skills at the same time.

Ethan Watrall and Jeff Siatro, *Head First Web Design: A Brain-Friendly Guide* (Shroff Publishers/O'Reilly, 2009).

W3Schools.com, HTML Tutorial, at http://www.w3schools.com/html/default.asp. This is a good introduction to HTML – but it's not a quick read.

Jon Duckett, *HTML & CSS: Design and Build Websites* (John Wiley & Sons, 2011). This is a great introduction to designing and building Web sites in HTML and CSS. No previous experience is required, and it's equally suitable for novices and Web veterans. Introduces HTML and CSS in a way that makes them very easy to understand. The text, together with beautiful illustrations, explains the fundamentals of Web site design. I wish I had had this book when I first started learning HTML and CSS.

Josh Hill, *HTML 5 and CSS3 in Simple Steps* (Prentice-Hall, 2011). A good introduction for beginners to HTML5 and CSS3. It has large, full-color screenshots so that you can easily follow along step by step.

Codecademy.com, Web Fundamentals," at http://codecademy.com/learn. Learn how to create a Web site using HTML and CSS online.

About the Author

Mitesh Dabhi is a self-taught print and Web designer from the north west of England. He has a range of passions which include all aspects of digital design, photography and anything related to the World Wide Web.

www.ingramcontent.com/pod-product-compliance
Lightning Source LLC
Chambersburg PA
CBHW041149050326
40689CB00004B/712

* 9 7 8 1 5 0 0 5 0 1 8 4 6 *